Her Master
in
Swaledale

The river Swale and the Kisdon Gorge.

Her Master's Walks in Swaledale

Stephen I. Robinson

BARLEY · PUBLISHING
2002

Barley Publishing
10 Mill Green View
Swarcliffe
Leeds LS14 5JT

www.hm-walks.co.uk
email: barley@hm-walks.co.uk

First published 1993
Revised 2002

ISBN 1 898550 04 2. 2nd revised edition
(ISBN 1 898550 00 X. 1st edition)

Maps reproduced from Ordnance Survey mapping on behalf of
The Controller of Her Majesty's Stationery Office
© Crown Copyright. Licence Number MC100016545.

Drawings by Andrew Haddelsey
Maps and photographs by Stephen I. Robinson

Printed in Great Britain by:
Impressions (Leeds) Limited
The Mint, Moor View, Leeds LS11 9NF
Telephone 0113 246 1075

Langthwaite, the capital of Arkengarthdale.

Contents

Paw-word by 'Her'

Firstly 'Her' is called Sherry, but I'm sometimes referred to as 'Little Un', 'Lass' and 'Sher'. I don't mind really, although I do object to being called 'Tubby'. Okay, I may have put on a little weight over the years, but so has he!

Secondly, I'm a smooth fox terrier and not, as many people think, a long legged Jack Russell. Don't get me wrong, I have nothing against them, in fact, some of my best friends are Jack Russells. Grrrr!

I was fortunate in my choice of master (*well, in some ways*). He has taken me all over this island and we have visited some of its most beautiful countryside. But, for me, our walks in Swaledale will always be treasured. I have many happy memories of the lovely hay meadows where I brushed my coat in the sweet smelling flowers; the woodland glades where I often found the scent of a rabbit; and the many thirst quenching rivers and streams with their spectacular waterfalls.

One thing that always amazes me is the amount of time it takes him to get ready for a walk, especially if it's raining. He puts on his waterproof coat and trousers, a silly hat and leggings, he certainly doesn't like getting wet! Whereas I'm quickly ready to go out as and when required, however, I do wear my waterproof coat sometimes.

Finally, without me he would not have had a title for his books!

Without you 'Little Un' there would not have been any books.

6

Introduction

Few places in Great Britain have been endowed with the beauty, character and history which can be found in the Yorkshire Dales. Every year the diverse scenery attracts many thousands of visitors, who are able to enjoy a sense of adventure and fulfilment. The area of the Yorkshire Dales National Park was designated in 1953 and established the following year.

The Yorkshire Dales is Britain's third largest National Park, spreading across 680 square miles (1765 sq. km). The variety of landscape includes heather-clad moorland, limestone scars, steep sided valleys, swift flowing rivers and plunging waterfalls. Pastimes such as angling, caving, climbing, cycling, horse riding, walking and watersports are all regularly enjoyed there. One objective of a National Park is to 'preserve and enhance the natural beauty of the area for the enjoyment of future generations'. Planning and development within the park are, therefore, carefully controlled by the National Park Authority.

The walks described in this guide explore the area's most spectacular dale. Lying on the northern frontier of the National Park is Swaledale, with its unrivalled scenery and secluded grandeur. Over many years of walking the dales, I've become more attracted to Swaledale than any other area, I will never tire of visiting this 'very special dale.'

Entering Swaledale is like travelling back in time. It has managed to retain a peaceful and unchanged outlook, helped by having only one major road passing through it (*the B6270*). Above Keld this is little more than a single track road in some places. Swaledale is now reserved mainly for sheep farming, but the former lead mining industry has left its mark throughout the dale, leaving behind a selection of impressive and interesting remains on the moors and side valleys. One legacy of the lead mining period is a network of tracks and packhorse trails, now used by many walkers. The Pennine Way and the Coast-to-Coast Walk both pass through Swaledale.

Some of the outstanding features of the dale are its meadows. Allowed to grow hay and farmed by traditional methods they are free of man-made fertilisers, permitting a large variety of wild flowers to grow. They in their turn have encouraged many species of butterflies, insects, birds and small mammals to visit the area. The meadows are at their best in June and early July when a feast of colour begins with yellow buttercups, followed by white pignut, blue cranesbill and many other flowers.

On the border between Cumbria and Yorkshire, two mountain ridges guard the north-west passage from Swaledale; Nine Standards Rigg 2170 feet (662m) and High Seat 2326 feet (709m). The High Seat ridge is the watershed of four rivers, the Cotter, the Eden, the Swale and the Ure. The Swale at this point is known as Birkdale Beck and the actual birth of the river Swale takes place 4 miles (6.5km) downstream when the waters of Birkdale Beck and Great Sleddale Beck merge. The river Swale is reputedly the swiftest flowing river in England. Its name is generally accepted to mean 'whirling, rushing river,' and after a heavy cloudburst its perpetual rapid flow can become a raging and dangerous torrent.

There are many things that I would like to add about this spectacular dale but sadly there is not enough space. Please enjoy the walks and take your time, I did.

Stephen I. Robinson,

July 2002.

Be Prepared!

Walking, arguably the most enjoyable of pastimes and undoubtedly one of the healthiest, can be tailored to meet the requirements of almost anyone.

Your preference might be for a gentle stroll of three to four miles along a quiet riverbank or woodland path, or perhaps a strenuous hill walk of ten miles or more. Whichever you choose, provided you are properly equipped, your walk will not only be safe but also more enjoyable. This does not mean taking everything including the kitchen sink! If you are a keen photographer a camera with spare films is essential. Binoculars are mandatory for birdwatchers. The artist needs his sketchbook and pencil. But remember, everything you take is extra weight to be carried.

What to wear and carry will depend on the season, the weather and good sense.

The items in the following lists are recommended, but think carefully about what to take. Some extra items may be needed on a hill walk which could be left behind when walking through the lower meadows. Due to our unpredictable climate, however, a spare wool sweater and waterproofs should always be carried. *(Items in italics could be used in warmer conditions.)*

TO WEAR

Strong walking boots or stout shoes
Thick woollen socks (two pairs)
Cotton shirt *or T-Shirt*
Walking breeches, trousers *or shorts*
(Never wear jeans, they lose their heat retention when wet.)
Woollen hat, balaclava *or sun hat*

TO CARRY

A small rucksack, thirty to forty litres in capacity, to carry the following:
Waterproof anorak or cagoule
Wool sweater or fibre pile jacket
Gloves, scarf
First aid kit, compass, whistle
Torch, pencil and note pad
Ordnance Survey map of the area
Emergency rations, survival bag
Water bottle with water
Food and snacks

OPTIONAL ITEMS

Camera and spare films, binoculars
Swiss army knife
Flask with tea, coffee, soup or other hot drink
Waterproof over-trousers, gaiters
Five to ten yards of thin cord
(Useful for temporary laces etc.)

Gunnerside and Gunnerside Bottoms.

About the Walks

The walks consist of a variety of landscapes from lush meadows and woodland to heather clad moors and limestone scars, with the remains of the lead mining industry adding their own austere beauty.

All of the walks follow circular routes ranging from 5¾ to 10 miles (9 to 16km). They begin from a car park where one is available, or at a place where it is possible to park safely without blocking farm gateways or causing inconvenience to others.

For this edition all the routes were surveyed between February and July 2002 and the maps have been amended where necessary. However, from time to time walls, fences and hedges may be removed, stiles and gates resited, new forestry established and buildings demolished. For this reason it is recommended that the relevant Ordnance Survey maps and a compass are carried. They will help to determine landmarks and find alternative routes where necessary.

Only the relevant area of the map has been used and then simplified so that only the walls, fences, buildings, rivers, roads and landmarks etc where the route passes through are included.

Each map has the route marked in red with numbered arrow pointers for each section of the route. These relate to the descriptive guide on the facing page, which includes a grid reference for each stage of the walk. When used together these features should help to avoid confusion, but common sense and some map reading experience are desirable.

The times given for completion of the walks are approximate and do not include any allowance for lunch breaks, photo stops or sightseeing. As a rule of thumb, adding one third of the stated time for stops should be sufficient. If accompanied by young children extra walking time will have to be allowed. Extended stays at any of the inns or tea shops *en route* should also be added to the time.

GUNNERSIDE GILL and BLAKETHWAITE DAMS

from Gunnerside 8 miles (13km)

Starting from the peaceful village of Gunnerside, this delightful walk explores the full length of one of the longest and narrowest side valleys in Swaledale.

Gunnerside was once described as 'The Klondyke of the Dale' because of its important lead mining industry, which thrived in the eighteenth and nineteenth centuries. The mines along Gunnerside Gill were some of the most profitable in Swaledale. With the decline of the lead mining industry, many of the villagers were forced to look for employment further afield. Some moved to the Durham coal mines, Lancashire cotton mills and West Riding woollen mills where work was plentiful, whilst others emigrated to America and Spain.

Leaving the village our path climbs steeply at first, gradually levelling out after we reach the bridleway at Jingle Pot Edge. Continuing along the side of Gunnerside Gill, the influence which the lead mines have had on the area becomes more apparent. This is evident from the many derelict buildings, flues, shafts and spoil heaps, set in a valley of cascading streams and limestone scars. However, far from spoiling the beauty of the area, they are considered by many to enhance it.

Descending from Botcher Gill the ruins of Blakethwaite smelt mill and peat store make their impression on the landscape. The smelt mill was built in 1820 to process ore from the rich Blakethwaite vein. The ruined furnace shop has four iron pillars, which once supported the arches over the ore furnaces. Behind the furnace would have been the water-wheel, used to drive the bellows. Across the stone slab bridge over the stream is the peat store which held a full year's supply of fuel for the furnaces. Peat was cut in the early summer and brought here to store until it dried out. The wide arches would have helped to maintain adequate ventilation.

The course of the flue, climbing 150 feet (46m) up the hillside, can still be seen, but the terminating chimney has gone. Flues allowed the poisonous smoke from the smelt mill to cool, depositing lead oxide onto the walls. These deposits were too precious to waste and were recovered by men crawling into the flue and scraping off the residue with cowl rakes, a tool similar in shape to a garden hoe. The work was often hazardous, especially when compounds of arsenic were present in the sulphurous fumes. Several men lost their lives after falling into the pit below where they were smothered by the heavy soot.

Further upstream, after passing the attractive Blakethwaite Force, are the long disused Blakethwaite dams. This is where water for use at the smelt mill was stored until it was needed. The lower dam has been breached and little remains, but the upper dam has fared rather better and still has an impressive water race. Unfortunately, the reservoir above is silted up.

From the dams our route passes a shooting hut belonging to the estate of Lord Peel. The views from this hut are excellent, especially of the gill. Looking back, the Blakethwaite dams can now be seen in the distance, with Rogan's Seat behind. After crossing an area of spoil heaps our path descends through open pastures to a well preserved lime kiln. This type of kiln was used mainly for burning limestone, producing lime for use as a fertiliser or to make mortar for building.

Many of the barns in this area date from the lead mining period. During the middle of the nineteenth century the average life expectancy of mine workers was forty-six. Although accidents claimed many lives, most died from breathing in dust leading to chest infections, damaged lungs and lead poisoning. In order to promote better health, the miners were encouraged to keep a smallholding with a few sheep and one or two cows.

During our steep descent to Gunnerside there are beautiful views of Swaledale and the village providing an excellent finish to the walk.

Start/Parking:	Gunnerside, in the village square near the literary institute or near the river bridge.
Location:	Gunnerside lies on the B6270 Richmond to Kirby Stephen road 6 miles (9.5km) west of Reeth.
Grid Ref:	951 982.
Distance:	8 miles (13km) circular. Allow 4 hrs.
OS Maps:	Explorer OL30 (1:25,000) or Landranger 98 and 91 (or) 98 and 92 (1:50,000).
Refreshments:	The King's Head Inn, The Ghyllfoot Tea Rooms.
Public Toilets:	Gunnerside, by the side of the King's Head Inn.
Other:	Post Office, Methodist chapel, literary institute, telephone, bus service.

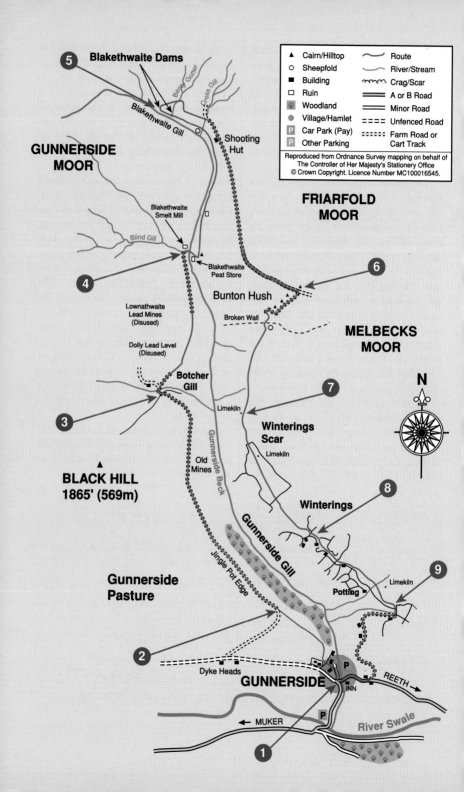

1 Gunnerside Gill and the Blakethwaite Dams

1 *(GR: 951 982)* Leave Gunnerside on a path climbing between South View and Rose Cottage, go through a gap stile and climb up a steep grassy bank.

2 *(GR: 945 987)* On reaching a wide bridlepath turn right. Follow this bridlepath along the side of the valley, rising gradually to arrive at Botcher Gill Gate.

3 *(GR: 935 006)* Go through the gate/stile and cross the bridge over Botcher Gill. Stay on the track to a bend and take a green track which leads off to the right *(SP Bridleway)*. Continue on this track passing the Dolly Lead Level and Lownathwaite Lead mines and descend to reach the Blakethwaite smelt mill and peat store.

4 *(GR: 937 018)* Cross Blind Gill and then Gunnerside Beck by the slab bridge, climb up a narrow track to a cairn, turn left and follow the beck upstream. After passing over two gills *(Cross Gill and Benty Gutter)* the Blakethwaite Dams are reached.

5 *(GR: 934 030)* Just above the dams, turn sharp right and head back to re-cross the two gills, to join a good stone track. After passing a shooting hut continue for about 1 mile on the stone track, through a rugged landscape of old mine workings. At a signpost on the right *(to Keld)* continue ahead on the stone track.

6 *(GR: 947 014)* On reaching a cairn turn sharp right and continue along a cairned track. As the track gets greener follow it round, descending towards a sheepfold and go through an open gateway in a broken wall. Continue to descend gradually towards Winterings Scar.

7 *(GR: 942 003)* After descending past an old limekiln turn left joining a broad green track, climb uphill briefly and through a gate into Winterings Pasture. The broad green track continues to Hugill House farm.

8 *(GR: 949 994)* Pass behind the farmhouse and continue on a stony farm track, which leads through a gate and past Whin House. Cross a beck above Pottings Farm and follow the track to a fork.

9 *(GR: 956 988)* Fork right and immediately go through a gate, joining a tarred track. Follow this as it winds its way down to go through a gate which leads onto the main road at Gunnerside. Turn right and follow the road back to the village centre.

MELBECKS MOOR and SURRENDER BRIDGE

from Gunnerside 9 miles (14.5km)

The contrast in scenery on this walk is superb. It begins with luxuriant woodland, sparkling streams and limestone scars before the devastation of the lead mining period is encountered. The paths were once used by miners as they trudged wearily to and from work.

Like many of the villages in Upper Swaledale, Gunnerside is of Norse origin, supposedly taking its name from a Viking warrior called Gunnar who settled in the valley at the start of the eleventh century.

The early part of the walk follows lovely beckside and woodland paths to the ruins of the Sir Francis crushing mill. Spoil heaps and a water-wheel pit are all that remain of the crushing mill. The row of bunkers seen here were known as bouse

teams and were used for storing the ore prior to crushing and washing. Each of the bunkers held the ore of one partnership of six to eight miners. The number of bunkers in a bouse team gives an indication as to the size of the mining operation and the number of miners who worked there.

From the crushing mill our path climbs high above the beck. Across the valley Jingle Pot Edge, Black Hill and Botcher Gill with its attractive waterfalls, make their contribution to this deep, confining valley.

Many of the huge gullies on the valley sides are the result of an early open cast mining technique known as 'hushing.' This involved the construction of a turf dam above the suspected vein. When sufficient water had been collected, it was released so that the sudden torrent swept down, tearing away the soil and exposing the vein. The miners then used picks and crowbars to loosen and remove the ore. This operation was carried out repeatedly, creating deep fissures in the hillside.

At Bunton Hush we join the Coast-to-Coast footpath and, after a scramble onto Melbecks Moor, the landscape becomes very bleak and austere. The ground is completely covered by gravel from the spoil heaps of the mines in the area. This is gradually being reclaimed, so the odd tractor may be seen. Continuing through the spoil heaps, we descend to cross Level House Bridge, and then follow the stream to the Old Gang smelt mill.

The remains of the smelt mill are impressive and well worth exploration. One prominent feature is the large intact chimney. The long building nearest the track is where the smelting took place. It used to have four ore furnaces, producing 2000 tons of lead per year. Much of the stone from these buildings was removed in the 1930s to build a new Methodist chapel at Muker.

On the moor above, the double row of pillars belonged to the peat store. This was an immense structure some 390 feet (119m) long and 21 feet (6.5m) wide, capable of storing enough peat for up to three year's smelting. The mill has recently undergone careful consolidation by English Heritage to prevent it from deteriorating further.

Our route continues alongside the stream to Surrender Bridge, and after a short climb on the road, the devastation caused by the mines is left behind. The scenery becomes less austere as we begin to cross Feetham Pasture, and the descent to the hamlet of Blades is quite stunning.

John Wesley preached at Blades on his first visit to Swaledale in 1761. In his journal Wesley wrote, "The Society is one of the most lively I have met in England." The area soon became a Methodist stronghold. Further along the hillside is the turning for Smarber, where the Puritan sympathiser Philip Lord Wharton allowed his shooting lodge at Smarber Hall to be used for Nonconformist worship.

We continue along a green bridlepath above the limestone terraces of Barf Side Scar. Looking towards the head of the dale there are excellent views of Great Shunner Fell and Muker. During our descent to Gunnerside, we have a bird's eye view of the field barns and walls in Gunnerside Bottoms. This patchwork of enclosures dates from the sixteenth century.

Start/Parking:	Gunnerside, in the village square near the literary institute or near the river bridge.
Location:	Gunnerside lies on the B6270 Richmond to Kirby Stephen road 6 miles (9.5km) west of Reeth.
Grid Ref:	951 982.
Distance:	9 miles (14.5km) circular. Allow 4¾ hrs.
OS Maps:	Explorer OL30 (1:25,000) or Landranger 98 and 92 (1:50,000).
Refreshments:	The King's Head Inn, The Ghyllfoot Tea Rooms.
Public Toilets:	Gunnerside, by the side of the King's Head Inn.
Other:	Post Office, Methodist chapel, literary institute, telephone, bus service.

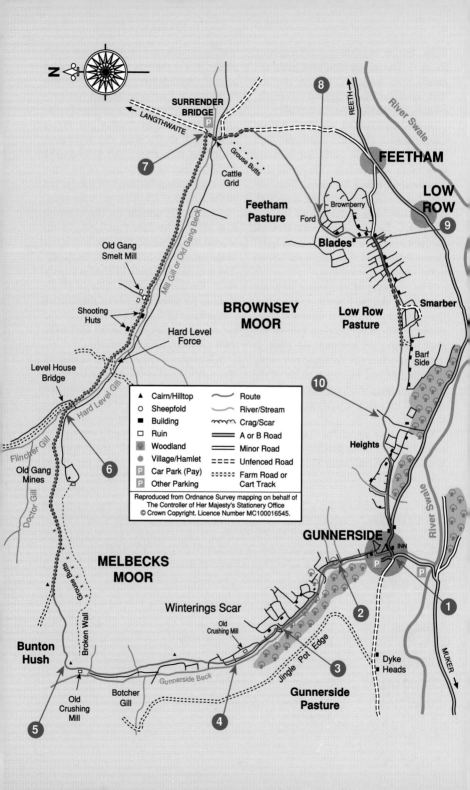

2 Melbecks Moor and Surrender Bridge

1 *(GR: 951 982)* Leave Gunnerside heading over the bridge towards Reeth and turn immediately left onto a track opposite the King's Head Inn *(SP Gunnerside Gill)*. Follow the track for about 150 yards (135m) to a large white gate, turn right and climb up some steps. Pass through a small gate, turning left to join a clear path, continue over a broken wall staying close to the beck side.

2 *(GR: 950 987)* Go through a gated stile and pass through a small wood. Continue along the beck side through an area with large boulders and after 300 yards (270m), go through a gated stile on the right, climb up some steps and continue to a signpost *(SP Gunnerside Gill Woodland Path)*. Follow the path over a wooden stile and through the wood.

3 *(GR: 944 993)* Leave the wood via two gap stiles and turn left. Stay with the left wall through two more gap stiles to reach the remains of the Sir Francis Crushing Mill. Keep to the left of the ruins, following the yellow waymarks.

4 *(GR: 941 998)* Cross a wooden step stile and follow a path up through the bracken. Go over another wooden step stile and through a gap stile to join a well defined track. Follow this track for about ¾ mile (1.2km) to reach the ruins of the Bunton Mines.

5 *(GR: 940 013)* 200 yards (180m) past the ruins, a cairn/signpost is reached. Turn right here *(SP Surrender Bridge)* and climb the Bunton Hush onto Melbecks Moor. *(This section is difficult to follow although nearer the top the route becomes obvious.)* At the top, head half left to reach a broad stone track. Turn right onto this track and follow it for about 1¾ miles (2.6km), passing through a line of grouse butts and the ruins of the Old Gang Lead Mine, to reach Flincher Gill.

6 *(GR: 964 013)* Cross the gill over Level House Bridge, turn right and go through a gate, joining Gruvers Trod *(an old miner's track)* with Hard Level Gill to the right. After about ¼ mile (400m) a slight detour right leads to Hard Level Force. Return to the stone track and continue for a further 1¼ miles (1.8km) passing two shooting huts and the Old Gang smelt mill. A gate leads onto the road at Surrender Bridge.

7 *(GR: 989 999)* Turn right and continue over Surrender Bridge. Follow the road over a cattle grid and climb steeply uphill At a footpath sign on the right leave the road and follow a clear green track across the moor. Continue along this track for about 1 mile (1.4km) across Feetham Pasture keeping right at a fork.

8 *(GR: 981 989)* After crossing a ford, go through a gate and continue downhill, staying on the track, to pass through the tiny hamlet of Blades.

9 *(GR: 980 984)* Turn right onto the road. When the tarmac surface becomes a concrete track, follow it to a bend *(which leads left to Smarber)*, continue straight ahead on a green bridlepath keeping to the left wall. When the wall ends continue on the same heading along the top of Barf Side Scar.

10 *(GR: 964 983)* After going through a wooden gate turn left, descend on a clear green path. The path becomes enclosed after passing by Heights. Continue descending, crossing over a beck to reach a tarmac lane, turn left and follow the lane downhill through a gate leading onto the main road at Gunnerside. Turn right and follow the road back to the village centre.

OXNOP GILL and IVELET BRIDGE

from Muker 7½ miles (12km)

This splendid walk explores the unspoilt side valley of Oxnop Gill. Route finding is easy, which allows more time to enjoy the exceptional views.

The attractive village of Muker is situated at the foot of Kisdon Hill. Its clusters of grey stone cottages huddle together above the beck, which joins the river Swale below the bridge to the east. Muker has several interesting buildings, including the literary institute of 1868, the old schoolhouse founded in 1687 and the prominent St Mary's Church.

The church was founded in 1580 as a chapel of ease under Grinton, which at that time had the only consecrated ground in Upper Swaledale. This was one of the few churches to be built in England during the reign of Elizabeth I. It was enlarged in 1761 with a higher roof and restored again in 1890 when the musicians' gallery was removed. The bells are thought to have been brought from Ellerton Priory after the Dissolution. The village used to have a communal coffin, this was carried to the churchyard, the corpse removed and the coffin was used again for the next funeral. This practice ceased in 1735, when the vicar decreed that all of his parishioners deserved the dignity of being buried in their own personal coffin.

Muker still holds an annual show on the first Wednesday in September, at which some of the finest Swaledale tups and ewes are on show. The origin of the show was most likely an annual fair which used to be held there called 'Muker Old Roy.' It

18

was so named because of the miners having a good spree, or 'roy' as it was known locally, after each fair. Muker's Silver Band, the 'Old Roy,' no doubt named after the fair, plays at the show throughout the day.

The walk begins with a crossing of the steep hillside to the road above Crow Trees Farm. Although narrow this road is fairly quiet and leads uphill, above Oxnop Gill to Oxnop Scar

Oxnop Gill is a deeply cut side valley, the lower part being a fine example of a gill wood. These woods are the remains of former birch forests, once covering the upper fells stretching to the open moor. In contrast the upper gill has some attractive waterfalls and the magnificent outcrop of Oxnop Scar. Along the top of the scar there are splendid views to Kisdon Hill and the fells beyond.

From Oxnop Scar we descend along a tarmac lane passing Gill Head, a long-house style farmhouse. These were built with a living area, a cow shed and a barn, all under one roof. Just below the farmhouse there is a beautiful panorama of the valley stretching from Muker to Gunnerside. Directly opposite, above the hamlet of Ivelet, is Gunnerside Lodge which belongs to Lord Peel, a local landowner.

After reaching Satron we continue on a meadow path leading to the river Swale and the highlight of our walk. The packhorse bridge at Ivelet, which has an attractive single-spanned high stone arch, was built in about 1695. The area around the bridge is so quiet that it is easy to imagine the packhorses laden with their heavy panniers crossing over the bridge and plodding their way along the peaceful, tree-shaded lane. According to local folk-lore, the area around this ancient bridge is haunted by a headless dog which brings bad luck to anyone who sees it. The dog is usually sighted gliding onto the bridge, where it disappears over the edge.

From the bridge we follow a clear path, never far from the riverside, through lush meadows back to Muker. The meadows are seen at their best during early summer, when the great variety of wild flowers seem to change their colour week by week. This is an area of outstanding natural beauty and has been designated as environment-ally sensitive.

On the opposite side of the river is the Yelland's Meadow Nature Reserve, belonging to the Yorkshire Wildlife Trust. The meadow is farmed by a local farmer using traditional methods.

Start/Parking:	Muker, there is a good sized car park by the bridge at the eastern end of the village.
Location:	Muker is situated 9 miles (14.5km) to the west of Reeth on the B6270 Richmond to Kirby Stephen road.
Grid Ref:	910 979.
Distance:	7½ miles (12km) circular. Allow 4 hrs.
OS Maps:	Explorer OL30 (1:25,000) or Landranger 98 (1:50,000).
Refreshments:	The Farmer's Arms, The Muker Store and Tea Shop, Muker Crafts.
Public Toilets:	Muker, on the main road opposite the Farmer's Arms.
Other:	Post Office, Swaledale Woollens, Muker Craft Shop, telephone, bus service.

IVELET and GUNNERSIDE

from Muker 6½ miles (10.5km)

Starting from the pretty village of Muker, this walk follows well defined paths and has a few easy climbs. There are superb views to be enjoyed on both outward and return journeys.

Muker, recorded as 'Meuhaker' in 1274, takes its name from the Norse for 'small cultivated field,' although some records show it to mean 'meadow'. The village grew up around the lead mining activities of the eighteenth and nineteenth centuries. During this period many people supplemented their income by knitting. Every member of the family would be involved, and merchants travelled across the dale leaving wool at the cottages and collecting the finished knitwear later. In the middle of the eighteenth century an estimated 18,000 pairs of stockings were produced each year in the Swaledale area. Woollen products had always been a valuable commodity and over the years deliberate efforts were made to establish a profitable cloth trade. In 1571, a statute ordered that knitted caps must be worn on Sundays and holidays, and an act of Charles II required all shrouds to be woollen.

This 'cottage industry' of hand knitting was revived in 1972, with the founding of Swaledale Woollens. Sweaters, caps, socks and jackets are created by over thirty knitters, using wool which has been spun from the local Swaledale sheep. Because of its resistance to cold and damp, Swaledale wool is valued by mountaineers and polar explorers.

The walk begins with a pleasant stroll through lush meadows to the river Swale, where there are appealing views of Kisdon Hill and the valley extending towards Swinner Gill. After crossing Rampsholme Bridge, we join a tarmac lane which leads all the way to Gunnerside. Along the way, we pass Gunnerside Lodge at Ivelet, the home of Lord Peel, who owns a substantial area of the grouse moors hereabouts.

The tranquil village of Gunnerside was developed from two quite individual communities; Lodge Green on the east side of the beck and Gunnerside on the west. Although now a single village it is still divided by Gunnerside Beck, which rushes down beside the road and swirls peacefully together with the river Swale. However, if in flood they compete for supremacy in a turbulent clash.

The most prominent building in Gunnerside is the large Methodist chapel. It was built in 1789, to hold a congregation of 500, making it one of the earliest Methodist chapels in Swaledale. The chapels were built with donations received from the miners, who would also have helped to transport the stone and materials from which the chapels were constructed. The mine owners approved of Methodism, or any belief that preached the virtues of hard work and sobriety. When John Wesley preached here in 1761 he received a warm welcome, prompting him to write, "The local congregation are an earnest, loving and simple people."

From Gunnerside our route passes through lush meadows to reach the river Swale at Marble Scar. There are fine views along the valley to Satron and Lovely Seat. We continue through the meadows, first to Ivelet and then to Calvert Houses.

Ivelet is a sedate little hamlet with a delightful waterfall which plunges 100 feet (30m) in three spectacular leaps. Calvert Houses was originally a much larger settlement, on a busy packhorse road, and even had its own inn. In the late sixteenth century, Richard Milner of Calvert Houses settled in Leeds where he became a successful merchant. One of his descendants, William Milner, served as Mayor of Leeds in 1697, and his son was created a baronet. The hamlet has some exceptional views of Muker Side, Kisdon Hill and Great Shunner Fell.

When the path returns to the riverbank we continue upstream to Rampsholme Bridge, where we follow the outward route back to Muker.

Start/Parking:	Muker, there is a good sized car park by the bridge at the eastern end of the village.
Location:	Muker is situated 9 miles (14.5km) to the west of Reeth on the B6270 Richmond to Kirby Stephen road.
Grid Ref:	910 979.
Distance:	6½ miles (10.5km) circular. Allow 3½ hrs.
OS Maps:	Explorer OL30 (1:25,000) or Landranger 98 and 92 (1:50,000).
Refreshments:	The Farmer's Arms , The Muker Store and Tea Shop, Muker Crafts at Muker. The King's Head Inn and Ghyllfoot Tea Rooms at Gunnerside.
Public Toilets:	Muker, on the main road opposite the Farmer's Arms, Gunnerside, by the side of the King's Head Inn.
Other:	Post Office, Swaledale Woollens, Muker Craft Shop, telephone, bus service.

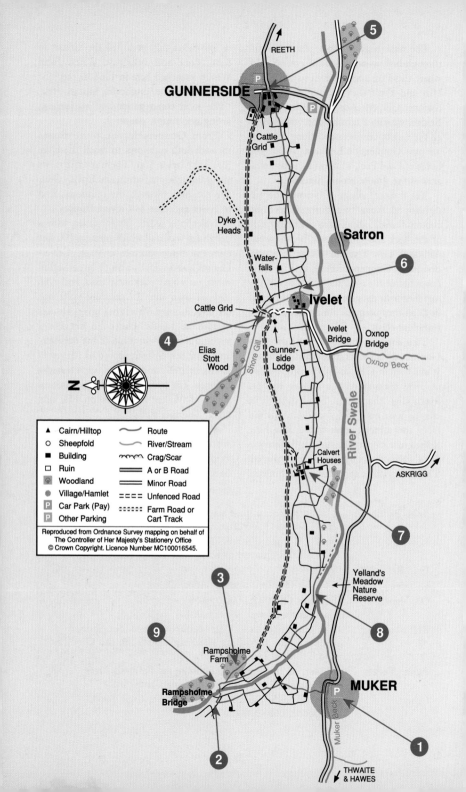

4 Ivelet and Gunnerside

1 *(GR: 910 979)* From the car park, cross the bridge and turn right before the village store, passing the church and village hall. Bear right and then left down a narrow lane leading to the Post Office, *(SP footpath to Gunnerside)* and continue through a gap stile. Follow a clear track through seven fields to reach the riverbank.

2 *(GR: 909 986)* Turn right here, go through a stile and cross Rampsholme Bridge. Climb up a few steps, turn right and follow the fence, continue to a fork (about 30 yards before a barn). Take the left path and climb up to join a wide track.

3 *(GR: 912 984)* Turn right and follow the track which soon becomes a tarmac road. Follow the road all the way to Gunnerside Lodge at Ivelet *(Gunnerside Lodge is the home of Lord Peel, a local landowner)*.

4 *(GR: 936 982)* Bear left, down over a bridge and cattle grid, climb back up and continue on the road. After crossing another cattle grid, the main road at Gunnerside is reached.

5 *(GR: 951 982)* Turn right and then first right *(after East View cottage)* which leads past the village school and through a gate on the right between the Flatlands housing area *(SP to Ivelet)*. Pass through four fields. At the fifth field, ignore the stile to the left and continue along the fence going through nine gap stiles, keeping roughly at the same level.

6 *(GR: 937 980)* When a beck is reached, cross by the footbridge and continue into Ivelet Village. Cross the road by the telephone box, go through the gate opposite and begin climbing up through a series of gap stiles to reach a farm *(Calvert Houses)*.

7 *(GR: 925 980)* After going through the gap stile into Calvert Houses continue across the farmyard and cross a step stile by another gate. Descend gradually through two gap stiles passing a small deciduous wood. Continue through three more gap stiles to join the riverbank briefly, merging with a path coming from the left at a signpost.

8 *(GR: 917 979)* Descend slightly and cross a step stile in the fence on the left. Follow the fence and go through a gap stile, continue via four more gap stiles to arrive at Rampsholme Farm. Pass to the front of the farmhouse, cross the meadow and go through another gap stile and then follow the wall/fence to Rampsholme Bridge.

9 *(GR: 911 986)* After crossing the bridge return by the outward route to Muker.

FREMINGTON EDGE, HURST and ARKLE BECK

from Reeth 7½ miles (12km)

The area explored during this walk has a good contrast of terrain and scenery; heather-clad moors, lead mines and a beautiful beckside return through the meadows and woodland of Arkengarthdale.

Reeth is the capital of Upper Swaledale, occupying the loveliest of positions below Calver Hill, with views of the surrounding hills and wild moorland. It is a very attractive village with a large sloping green, enclosed on each side by housing, hotels and shops. Reeth used to be a busy market town with a charter granted in 1695 permitting four fairs each year and a market every Friday. The fairs and the market have long since gone, but the Annual Agricultural Show is still held on the last Wednesday in August.

After leaving Reeth a meadow path is followed to Fremington, a peaceful little village with its small scattering of stone cottages dotted about on the hillside. Most of the drystone walls which extend straight to the top of the fell are the result of the Parliamentary Enclosure Act of 1778. Enclosure of land for the purpose of scientific management was recommended by Sir Thomas Elliot of Fremington, one of the greatest improvers of the moors in Yorkshire. He advised "never to attempt any improvement without enclosing". This action transformed the countryside and contributed to the unique character of the Dales.

From Fremington we follow a narrow tarmac lane which climbs up behind the aptly named White House passing some former chert quarries to Fremington Edge. Chert is a hard, flint-like stone, which was quarried in both black and white forms. It was ground to a fine powder and used in the making of fine china and pottery. As height is gained we are favoured with splendid views of Reeth, Arkengarthdale and Swaledale. Our route continues across the heather covered Marrick Moor to the ancient hamlet of Hurst, with its two imposing chimneys.

The isolation of Hurst provides an introduction to the bleak and rugged landscape, created by the lead mining industry in the eighteenth and nineteenth centuries. During the time of the Roman occupation, the Hurst mines are thought to have been used as a penal settlement, where slaves and convicts were sent to work. Lead from Hurst is said to have been used to roof buildings in Jerusalem and St Peter's in Rome.

The village was once known as Red Hurst owing to the discoloured waters of a nearby spring and Redshanks was the nickname of the Hurst men. According to legend, a traveller was passing by the spring when the guardian spirit snatched him up, dyeing the spring with his blood. The villagers went to pray for his soul and saw a vision of the Virgin, thereafter the Well of Roan "flourished with blessings and streamed with health".

Our route from Hurst passes through a large area of mining spoil to reach the cairns at Fell End. Here spectacular views extend across Arkengarthdale to the tiny hamlet of Booze and the more prominent landmark of North Rake Hush over the side valley of Slei Gill. From the cairns we descend to the delightfully positioned cottage of Storthwaite Hall, which sounds very grand but the translation means 'the bullock clearing'.

The return along Arkle Beck has to be the highlight of the walk, with beautiful woodland, lush meadows and superb views to enjoy all the way.

Arkle Beck rises on the wild moorland near the Tan Hill Inn. It is a fast flowing tributary to the river Swale which it joins near Grinton Bridge. Do not be misled by the gentle look of Arkle Beck. In 1986 when 'Hurricane Charley' passed, it became a powerful and destructive force rising 12 feet (3.5m) above normal. Further upstream, the top of Whaw's bridge was washed away and cottages at Langthwaite were flooded to a depth of 2 feet (0.6m) on the ground floors.

Start/Parking:	Reeth, around the village green and also an overflow car park 100 yards (90m) along the Gunnerside road.
Location:	Reeth is 11 miles (17.5km) from Richmond on the B6270 Richmond to Kirby Stephen road.
Grid Ref:	038 993.
Distance:	7½ miles (12km) circular. Allow 4 hrs.
OS Maps:	Explorer OL30 (1:25,000) or Landranger 98 and 92 (1:50,000).
Refreshments:	The Black Bull, The Buck Hotel, The King's Arms, The Copper Kettle Restaurant, The Cobbles Tea Shop
Public Toilets:	Reeth, near the Buck Hotel.
Other:	Swaledale Folk Museum, Blacksmith's Ceramic Design, Reeth Gallery, Philip Bastow's, Post Office, telephone, bus service.

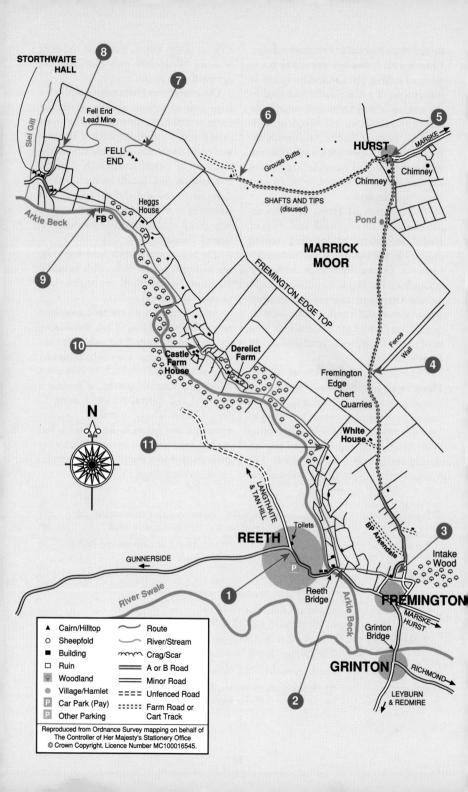

5 Fremington Edge, Hurst and Arkle Beck

1 *(GR: 038 993)* Leave Reeth via the Richmond Road and after crossing the bridge over Arkle Beck, go through a stile on the left.

2 *(GR: 042 992)* Take the right path through a stile, then bear left to another stile to the right of an iron gate. Turn right and stay with the wall through two more gap stiles, emerging onto a road at High Fremington.

3 *(GR: 046 991)* At the first cottage on the left *(Brambles)*, turn left onto an enclosed track and follow it uphill to join a narrow tarmac lane. Turn left and keep on this lane, climbing uphill to a gate. From the gate, continue up to a fork where the tarmac lane changes to a stony track by a spring. Follow the right fork, passing behind the White House. Ignore public footpath signpost and continue to climb up via a gate, passing some old chert quarries. Ignore all forks and climb up to the gate in the wall at the top.

4 *(GR: 044 007)* Go through the gate and continue on a stone track which leads directly away from the wall and across Marrick Moor, to the hamlet of Hurst. After going through a gate Hurst's two chimneys are very prominent.

5 *(GR: 046 023)* Go through a gate onto the road. Turn left and continue via two gates to join a clear stone track which leads across the mining spoil. After passing through a line of grouse butts, the track becomes a little greener. Follow it round to the left and uphill to a right bend, where a wall comes into view *(Fremington Edge Top)*.

6 *(GR: 034 021)* At a cairn on the left, leave the track and follow a path through a break in the heather. Head towards the wall and go through a gate where two wall corners meet. From the gate, a faint path leads towards some mining spoil heaps. Pass to the left of the spoil towards a cairn.

7 *(GR: 026 024)* From the cairn[1] the path descends through the mining spoil on a cairned/waymarked track and then winds down a stony section to arrive at a gate.

8 *(GR: 019 024)* Go through the gate *(SP Langthwaite)* and staying with the wall follow the blue waymarks down past Storthwaite Hall and through a gate onto a farm lane. Turn left, go through a gate and follow an enclosed lane to a farm, go through another gate. Continue across two meadows, dropping down to join Arkle Beck by a footbridge *(don't cross the bridge)*.

9 *(GR: 022 019)* Using the gate to the left of the bridge enter a small wooded area. At a fork, take the path to the right *(SP Footpath Reeth)* and follow the yellow waymarks over derelict walls. After entering another wood, continue to follow the yellow waymarks, cross a small stream and leave the wood, climbing up to a signpost. Turn right here and, after going through an open gateway *(SP Fremington)* head to the right hand wall. Cross over two broken walls, a farm track and through a gap stile to Castle House Farm.

10 *(GR: 030 009)* Pass behind the farmhouse, keeping to the wall. Cross an enclosed lane and over a broken wall opposite. Continue on an obvious track through a gap stile. Descend over two broken walls to a ruined farm. Arkle Beck is rejoined at the next wallcorner. Continue through an open gateway and, at a fork, follow the left track climbing away from the beck. Keep to the wall through three more open gateways.

11 *(GR: 041 001)* When the clear path fades out, go through a gap stile in the wall on the right. Descend to the right of a barn, through two stiles, then turn left through another stile. Keep to the right hand wall across two fields, to reach the stile at Reeth Bridge and then return to the car.

1. A detour is recommended to the left, along a narrow path which leads to the cairns on the cliffs at Fell End. Excellent views down the valley. Then retrace steps to cairn.

LANGTHWAITE via FORE GILL GATE

from Reeth 8 miles (13km)

This walk is a real tonic, yielding spectacular views of Swaledale and Arkengarthdale. The hills of Harkerside, Blea Barf, Muker Side and Brownsey Moor are visible almost from the start. The route uses moorland, beckside and meadow paths.

The valley divides at Reeth, with the narrow sided Swaledale heading west and the wide, open valley of Arkengarthdale climbing north west towards Tan Hill. This area was written off as wasteland by the Normans when they were compiling the Domesday Book in 1086.

From Reeth the ancient track of Skelgate Lane leads up to the open moor, where a broad track traverses the lower slopes of Calver Hill, also known locally as Mount Calva. The name is believed to

have a religious background, and some of the local people have carried on the tradition of having their ashes scattered there. In 1937 one man actually had a cross built close to the summit. It is named Gobat's Cross after him.

On the descent to Moorcock House there is a bird's eye view of Healaugh, and, as height is regained, the Old Gang valley and Surrender Bridge come into view. Straight ahead in the far distance are the remains of the Stokoe condenser chimney. This was part of the Surrender smelt mill's flue system. Its purpose was to trap the poisonous flue gases and extract the lead by condensing it onto the walls of the flue. The flue was cleaned at regular intervals by men, who had to crawl inside and scrape off the 'lead rich' soot from the walls.

A feeling of *déjà vu* may be experienced at Fore Gill Gate, the now famous water-splash having featured in the popular television series *All Creatures Great and Small*. James Herriot, the veterinary surgeon, was seen driving through the water-splash, a scene often recreated by the programme's many fans.

The road from Langthwaite to Low Row, passing Fore Gill Gate, was one of the main drove roads through Swaledale. Every year many thousands of cattle were driven south on foot from the Scottish Highlands to feed the industrial towns of England. This method of transporting cattle survived until the 1890s. With the introduction of refrigeration, animals were slaughtered locally and the meat itself was distributed where it was most needed.

After a short walk along the road, the panorama of Arkengarthdale unfolds. Kitley Hill, Booze Moor, and Fremington Edge form a magnificent backdrop to the villages of Langthwaite and Arkle Town, nestling in the valley below.

Arkengarthdale was named after Arkil, the son of Gospatrick, who held the estate before the conquest. In 1071, William the Conqueror gave Arkengarthdale, along with the Honour of Richmond, to Alan Rufus of Brittany. It remained in the possession of successive earls until 1435, when it reverted to the Crown.

Arkle Town was the site of Arkengarthdale's first church built in 1145. The foundations were undermined by the beck and it was demolished in 1818, replaced by the church at Langthwaite. Its grave-yard still exists with some forlorn old tombstones all sloping at different angles.

The church of St Mary, further up the main road, was built around 1818 to give thanks for the victory over Napoleon at the Battle of Waterloo. Churches built to commemorate this victory are known as 'Waterloo Churches'. Their design was strictly regulated and they had to represent good value for money. Robert Thompson, the 'Mouseman' of Kilburn, carved the reredos and altar table which bear his famous mouse trademark.

Langthwaite's small village square is reached over an ancient bridge. Its tiny stone cottages and the Red Lion Inn are crowded together at the foot of the steep hillside. The name is of Scandinavian origin and means 'the long clearing'.

From Langthwaite the delightful Arkle Beck and luxuriant meadows provide an enjoyable finish to the walk.

Start/Parking:	Reeth, around the village green and also an overflow car park 100 yards (90m) along the Gunnerside road.
Location:	Reeth is 11 miles (17.5km) from Richmond on the B6270 Richmond to Kirby Stephen road.
Grid Ref:	038 993.
Distance:	8 miles (13km) circular. Allow 4 hrs.
OS Maps:	Explorer OL30 (1:25,000) or Landranger 98 and 92 (1:50,000).
Refreshments:	The Black Bull, The Buck Hotel, The King's Arms, The Copper Kettle Restaurant, The Cobbles Tea Shop at Reeth. The Red Lion Inn and The Charles Bathurst Hotel at Langthwaite.
Public Toilets:	Reeth and Langthwaite.
Other:	Swaledale Folk Museum, Blacksmith's Ceramic Design, Reeth Gallery, Philip Bastow's, Post Office, telephone, bus service.

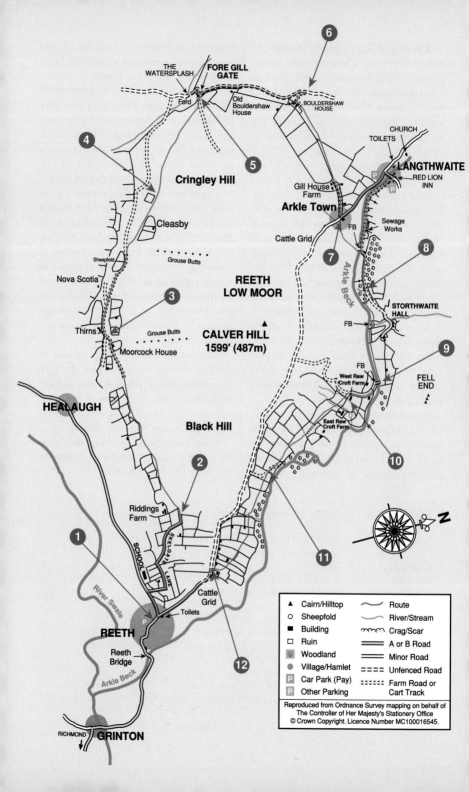

6 Langthwaite via Fore Gill Gate

1 *(GR: 038 993)* Leave Reeth on the Gunnerside road, climbing up School Hill. About 150 yards (135m) after the last house on the right, turn right onto a narrow enclosed lane *(SP Skellgate)*. Follow the lane for about ¾ mile (1.2km) to its end at a wooden gate which leads onto the open moor.

2 *(GR: 029 998)* Go through the gate, follow the left wall to its corner then head towards a cairn. Continue on the track, rejoining the wall after about 150 yards (135m). When the track becomes broader and stony, bear left at a fork and descend, *(just after passing a three way signpost)* passed Moorcock House, to reach Thirns Farm.

3 *(GR: 012 995)* Turn right and follow a rough track close to the wall. At a fork take the right track and climb up again, passing above a large sheepfold. After the sheepfold, leave the stony track along a waymarked path on the right towards the wall of Cleasby *(a three field enclosure)*. Continue just below the wall and when a wire fenced enclosure is reached, pass to the right of it, staying on the faint path.

4 *(GR: 001 003)* At the end of the enclosure join a green track and continue climbing, to follow the shoulder of Cringley Hill. Stay on the track to a wall *(The watersplash can be seen below)*. After joining a clearer track from the right, a gate leads onto the road just above a double bend. *(This is Fore Gill Gate.)*

5 *(GR: 993 009)* A brief detour downhill to the left takes in the now famous watersplash. Retrace steps and follow the road uphill.

6 *(GR: 995 019)* After just over ½ mile (800m), turn right onto a farm track, down to Bouldershaw House Farm. At the farm, turn left and follow the wall to its corner then, keeping roughly the same distance from the wall, descend through a gate. Return to the right wall and pass Gill House Farm *(The Ghyll)* to join a stony track. After going through a gate at the aptly named White House, the road in Arkle Town is soon reached.

7 *(GR: 007 019)* Turn left towards Langthwaite, then take the first right at Langthwaite and cross the bridge over Arkle Beck. At the Red Lion Inn, turn right onto a lane opposite, then bear right to join a cart track and follow the beck downstream. On reaching a footbridge, the track bears left to run along the bottom edge of a wood.

8 *(GR: 014 020)* At a fork, bear right heading back towards the beckside. Leave the wood through a tunnel with a gated stile, go through a gap stile and cross Slei Gill over a footbridge. Proceed through a gate, over a wooden stile and two meadows, keeping to the beckside, to arrive at a footbridge.

9 *(GR: 022 019)* Cross the footbridge, follow the beck downstream and go through a gate. Continue along an enclosed green track uphill and go through a gate leading to West Raw Croft Farm,

10 *(GR: 023 016)* Turn left in front of the farm, over a spring and through a gate. Continue through a gap stile, staying close to the left wall. Follow the yellow waymarks through a gate and two gap stiles to join a farm track.

11 *(GR: 028 007)* Follow the track through a gate, bear left, leaving the track, to go through an open gateway. Continue through a gap stile, follow a derelict wall passing a waymarked telephone pole, to a signpost by a tree *(Langthwaite/Reeth)*. This points the way over a beck and through nine gap stiles, well waymarked in yellow, to reach the road.

12 *(GR: 035 000)* Turn left and follow the road over a cattle grid and ½ mile (800m) back to Reeth.

MARRICK PRIORY and FREMINGTON EDGE

from Reeth 7½ miles (12km)

This pleasant walk begins with a gentle stroll alongside Arkle Beck and the river Swale. The varied scenery of meadows, luxuriant woodland and heather-clad moorland enables the full beauty of Swaledale to be appreciated.

Before leaving Reeth, a visit to the Swaledale Folk Museum is worthwhile. The museum was founded in 1973 and occupies the former Methodist Sunday school. Well laid out displays explain life in the dale; the lead mines, hand knitting, farming and much more.

Reeth Bridge was built in 1773 to replace one destroyed by the great flood of two years earlier. It was constructed by bridge master John Carr of York, who was also responsible for the rebuilding of the Downholme and Richmond bridges destroyed by the same flood.

After crossing the bridge we join a beckside path leading to Grinton. It passes Fremington Mill, where corn was ground by waterpower until the end of the nineteenth century. The water-wheel is almost intact. Grinton is an attractive village on the south side of the river Swale, the church and the inn facing each other beside the bridge. The rest of the village stretches uphill away from the busy main road.

St Andrew's Church is often referred to as 'The Cathedral of the Dales' because of its great age and grandeur. It was founded in the early twelfth century by the Augustinian Canons of Bridlington Priory. Most of the present church dates from the fifteenth and sixteenth centuries. It was restored in 1896. There is a lepers' squint in the south chapel, where lepers would have taken turns to watch the church services. Grinton was one of the largest parishes in the country. Being the only consecrated ground in Upper Swaledale, all corpses had to be brought here for burial. They were carried in wicker baskets along a route known as the 'Corpse Road'.

Our walk continues along riverside and meadow paths to Marrick Priory. The Priory of St Andrew was founded by Roger de Aske in 1154 as a house for Benedictine Nuns. It was dissolved in 1540 and all that remains of the original structure is the tower. The nave was rebuilt in 1811. The priory now serves as an outdoor pursuits and recreational centre for the Diocese of Ripon and Leeds.

Turner, the artist, visited the priory in 1816, making sketches for his grand *Histories of Yorkshire and Durham.* He forded the Swale near to the priory. During his tour through Northern England, Turner made more than 400 drawings, capturing almost every village, castle, abbey and waterfall along the way. In his tireless search for subjects he often travelled 25 miles (40km) a day. A series of seats are placed at some of the locations he visited, one is sited near the entrance to Steps Wood.

From the priory a flagged path known as the Nuns' Causey, climbs up through Steps Wood to Marrick. The Causey is supposed to have 375 steps, although many are rough and difficult to distinguish. Marrick is situated high on the hillside standing at just over 1000 feet (305m), where there are splendid views of Lower Swaledale and its beautiful woodland.

We follow the road out of Marrick, and at the junction a moorland track continues along Fremington Edge. The track passes above Jabez Cave. In the 1890s, Reeth shopkeeper and poet, Jabez Raisbeck, often retired to this tranquil spot to write his verses. During the descent to Fremington there are excellent views of Arkengarthdale and Swaledale, with Reeth sitting snugly at the foot of Calver Hill.

Fremington once had a school which served the whole of Grinton parish. It was founded in 1643 by James Hutchinson, a merchant and alderman of York, who was a native of Fremington. The school was mixed with an average attendance of sixty eight, but in 1811 there were 130 scholars.

After a short stroll across the meadows we return to Reeth Bridge.

Start/Parking:	Reeth, around the village green and also an overflow car park 100 yards (90m) along the Gunnerside road.
Location:	Reeth is 11 miles (17.5km) from Richmond on the B6270 Richmond to Kirby Stephen road.
Grid Ref:	038 993.
Distance:	7½ miles (12km) circular. Allow 4 hrs.
OS Maps:	Explorer OL30 (1:25,000) or Landranger 98 and 92 (1:50,000).
Refreshments:	The Black Bull, The Buck Hotel, The King's Arms, The Copper Kettle Restaurant, The Cobbles Tea Shop at Reeth. The Bridge Inn at Grinton.
Public Toilets:	Reeth, near the Buck Hotel.
Other:	Swaledale Folk Museum, Blacksmith's Ceramic Design, Reeth Gallery, Philip Bastow's, Post Office, telephone, bus service.

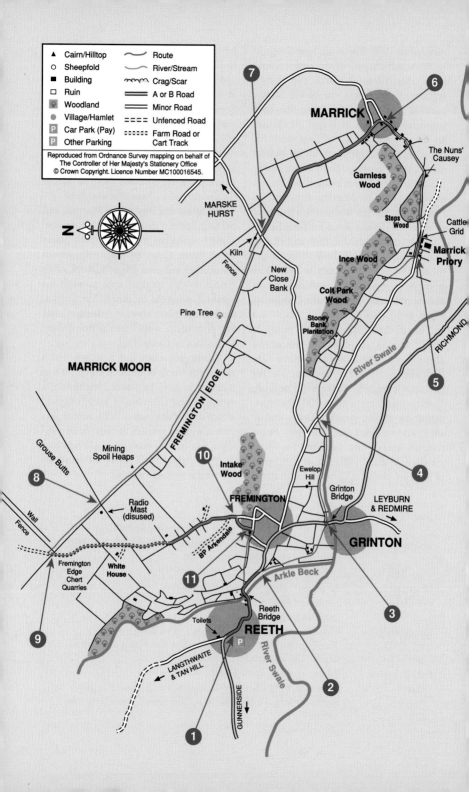

7 Marrick Priory and Fremington Edge

1 *(GR: 038 993)* Leave Reeth by the Richmond road. After crossing the bridge over Arkle Beck, follow the road for about 150 yards (135m).

2 *(GR: 043 991)* Go through a gate on the right *(SP Grinton)* to join the beckside. Pass some farm buildings and through a gate, leaving the beck to follow the path to the left. Go round a wallcorner, past some static caravans and go through two gates to reach Grinton Bridge.

3 *(GR: 046 986)* Cross the road, head to the left side of the bridge, where a path leads down to the river. Follow this path over two stiles, then climb up to a gate which emerges onto a tarmac road.

4 *(GR: 054 986)* Cross the road and go over a wooden stile. Then, climbing up, head half right to go through a stile in a fence. Continue through four fields staying close to the right fence/wall. From the ladder stile continue through two meadows towards the tower of Marrick Priory. After going through a gap stile, pass to the right of a fenced enclosure and go through a gate to rejoin the road at Marrick Priory.

5 *(GR: 066 979)* Turn left on the road, cross a cattle grid to join a farm track and turn left through a gate *(SP Marrick ¾)*. Climb a broad green path to a gate leading into Steps Wood and climb a flagged path *(the Nuns' Causey)* through the wood. Leave the wood through a gate/stile, keep to the wall on the right and follow a clear path through three gates. On the left is a former Wesleyan Chapel, dated 1878, continue along the lane to a road junction.

6 *(GR: 076 981)* At the junction, turn left and follow the road to a T-Junction. *(Reeth/Marske)*

7 *(GR: 068 991)* Cross the road to go through a gap stile in the wall opposite. Go through a gate in the top right corner of the field and follow the wall through another gate/stile in a fence. Keep to the wall and, climbing gradually past a lone pine tree, join a broad path along the top of Fremington Edge.

8 *(GR: 048 003)* After passing some spoil heaps, cross a ladder stile by a disused radio mast and then a wooden stile in a fence.

9 *(GR: 044 007)* Go through the gate on the left, follow a green track and begin to descend. After passing some old chert quarries and going through a gate, the track becomes stonier. Continue, passing behind the White House, where the track has a tarmac surface. Continue descending and go through a gate, stay on the road, passing a bridlepath on the right *(SP Arkendale 4m)*.

10 *(GR: 047 992)* Turn right onto a narrow walled track and follow it down past a cottage, returning to the road.

11 *(GR: 046 991)* Turn right onto the road, leaving it after a few yards by a track to the right. Go through the gap stile by the gate and continue along the wall through an open gateway and a gap stile. Go through a gap stile in the left wall, head half right through two more gap stiles to the road at Reeth bridge. From here return to the car park at Reeth.

THE TAN HILL INN and RAVENSEAT

from Keld 10 miles (16km)

Two well-known footpaths are used during this strenuous hill walk, crossing wild moorland and peat bogs with a pleasant riverside return. Exceptional panoramic views and refreshments at the Tan Hill Inn are among the rewards.

Situated at the head of the dale, Keld is the last settlement of any size in Swaledale. It takes its name from the Norse 'Kelda' meaning spring or stream, which is very apt because Keld is abundant with water. Wain Wath Force, East Gill Force, Catrake Force and the spectacular Kisdon Force are all within a short distance of the village.

In the 1890s Richard Alderson, known locally as 'Neddy Dick,' was climbing near Kisdon Force when he dislodged a rock. This struck another rock with a musical

sound. Realising different stones produced different notes of music, he scoured the bed of the river Swale for other melodious stones. Eventually he created his own 'heavy rock band' which he played with two wooden sticks. Neddy was encouraged by the local community and even made plans for a tour of the country. Sadly, he died just a few days before his debut.

After leaving Keld, the Pennine Way is joined. It passes the attractive East Gill Force and leads to the farmyard at East Stonesdale. From here we follow a moorland track to the Tan Hill Inn, which is England's highest inn, standing at 1732 feet (528m) above sea level.

Tan Hill Inn is surrounded by a bleak moorland wilderness 4½ miles (7km) from Keld, the nearest village. Tan Hill has not always been so isolated. It was on the crossroads of packhorse routes and drove roads. Later the Reeth to Brough turnpike was built to transport coal from the mines close by. Coal was mined at Tan Hill from the thirteenth century until 1932. The inn was once known as the King's Pit House, taking its name from a nearby coal pit. Licensing hours were at times dictated by need rather than the law. "Refuse no-one at Tan Hill," the justices ordered one landlord.

It is probably most famous for having featured in a television commercial for Everest Double Glazing, with the late Ted Moult. After walking through high winds to the inn and dropping a feather inside the newly installed windows, he picked up a pint and said, "This is the only draught you get up here." The same feather is displayed with his photograph above the bar.

Tan Hill still hosts an annual sheep fair which takes place on the last Thursday in May, when farmers from as far away as Scotland attend. The top prizes may only be a few pounds at Tan Hill, but the prestige of winning best of class can increase the selling price at a later auction. A tup hogg (young ram) was sold at Hawes' market for £30,000 after the 1990 show.

From the inn an old jagger, or coal road, is followed, climbing up Thomas Gill Hill and Robert's Seat to the ruined Robert's Seat House, a gamekeeper's shelter. Gamekeeping was a hazardous job, the poachers knew the moors well and if necessary would turn their guns on the keeper to avoid being caught.

There are outstanding views of Rogan's Seat, Lovely Seat and Great Shunner Fell, with Kisdon Hill in the foreground. Before descending to Ravenseat, look back for a distant view of the Tan Hill Inn.

Ravenseat is a tiny hamlet with a lovely stone-arched packhorse bridge. At one time eleven families lived here, sufficient to justify a public house and a small chapel. Most of the men worked in the coal mines at Tan Hill and they would have travelled the jagger road twice each day in all weathers, often soaked and chilled to the bone. During World War I, Ravenseat's farmers were ordered to grow corn, to help the war effort. They were still waiting for the corn to ripen in late November.

Leaving Ravenseat we follow the Coast-to-Coast footpath, first beside Whitsundale Beck and then the river Swale, returning to Keld. Some of Swaledale's loveliest waterfalls are passed along the way.

Start/Parking:	Keld village square. There is ample car parking available at Park Lodge Farm just off the village square.
Location:	Keld lies on the B6270 Richmond to Kirby Stephen road 12 miles (19km) west of Reeth.
Grid Ref:	893 012.
Distance:	10 miles (16km) circular. Allow 6 hrs.
OS Maps:	Explorer OL30 (1:25,000) or Landranger 91 (1:50,000).
Refreshments:	Park Lodge Farmhouse at Keld and The Tan Hill Inn.
Public Toilets:	Keld, half way between the road junction and the village square, and the Tan Hill Inn.
Other:	The United Reform Church, youth hostel, telephone, bus service.

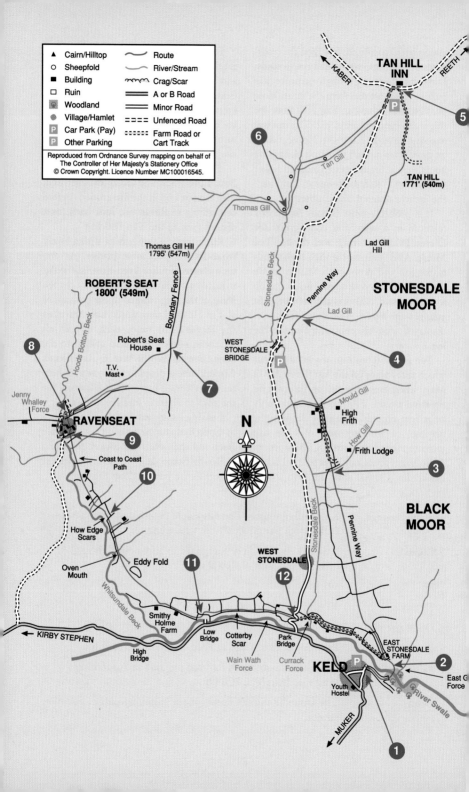

1 *(GR: 893 012)* Leave Keld at the bottom right of the village *(SP Public Footpath to Muker)*. After ½ mile (800m), turn left *(SP Pennine Way)*, follow the path down through a gate and cross the river Swale over a footbridge. Climb up the track to the left, passing by East Gill Force on the right.

2 *(GR: 896 011)* At a junction of paths *(PW and C to C)* turn left and climb up a track to East Stonesdale Farm. Go through the farmyard taking the right fork, *(Pennine Way)* then through a gate and along an enclosed track. At the end of the track a gate leads onto the open moor. Continue on a clear track through two gates, rising gradually along the side of Black Moor, to where the track starts to level out.

3 *(GR: 890 030)* Cross How Gill, go through a gate and continue along the path which soon joins a good stone track *(Frith Lodge to the right)*. Go through three gates and cross Mould Gill. The stone track ends here, continue across the moor to Lad Gill. *(The path is a little vague in places, but there are Pennine Way signposts at intervals.)*

4 *(GR: 887 045)* Cross the slab bridge at Lad Gill and head right, following a cairned track up Lad Gill Hill. When the track levels out and becomes broader, take a right fork marked by two cairns *(SP Pennine Way)*. Continue over Stonesdale Moor to Tan Hill, where a clear track is joined leading to the Tan Hill Inn.

5 *(GR: 897 067)* Turn left at the inn and left at the road junction towards Keld. Stay on the road to a signpost *(Ravenseat 3 miles)* and leave the road along a sketchy path, keeping Tan Gill to the left, descend to a merging of streams. Cross Tan Gill and continue along the left side of Stonesdale beck.

6 *(GR: 895 066)* Continue past two sheepfolds and cross Stonesdale Beck via a ford *(SP footpath)*. Keeping to the left of Thomas Gill, continue uphill to where it divides. Bear left *(SP footpath)* and continue along the rim of Thomas Gill towards a boundary fence and follow it round to a stile.

7 *(GR: 871 040)* Cross the stile *(SP footpath)* and continue past the ruins of Robert's Seat House. Head for a TV mast and descend to the left to cross a waymarked stile. Follow the waymark posts to cross another stile.

8 *(GR: 863 036)* **CHOICE OF ROUTES HERE**
Go through a gate on the left and continue downstream to Ravenseat, pass through a gap stile into the farmyard. Cross the farmyard to a stile in the wall opposite. **OR**

Continue to cross Hoods Bottom Beck via a ford at Jenny Whalley Force. Head downstream to Ravenseat via three gates. After passing the farmhouse turn left and cross a wooden bridge. Pass through a gate into the farmyard head to a stile in the right wall.

9 *(GR: 863 034)* Go through the stile *(SP Keld)*, staying parallel to Whitsundale Beck continue through another stile and past a waterfall. Go through a gate, climb up to the left *(SP footpath)* and pass to the right of two barns. Follow waymarks through two pastures to reach the How Edge Scars.

10 *(GR: 867 026)* Continue through three more gates to Oven Mouth Gorge. When the path forks take the lower right hand path which passes along the bottom of Eddy Fold, a large sheepfold. After passing the fold descend to the right towards Smithy Holme Farm. Join a stone track and follow it through two gates.

11 *(GR: 877 016)* Go through a gap in the left wall, turn right and follow the wall along the top of Cotterby Scar. Cross two ladder stiles and go through two gates to emerge onto the road above Park Bridge.

12 *(GR: 886 016)* Turn right, cross the road and go through a gate on the bend opposite *(sign East Stonesdale Farm)*. Follow a farm road down through a gate and over a bridge at Currack Force. Continue via three more gates to the farmyard at East Stonesdale, bear right and go through the gate, returning to Keld by the outward route.

9

KISDON HILL, THWAITE and MUKER

from Keld 6¾ miles (11km)

This spectacular walk from Keld provides excellent views of the surrounding heather moors and mountains; Lovely Seat, Great Shunner Fell, High Seat and Nine Standards Rigg, all above 2000 feet. The riverside return is stunning.

Keld is a most enchanting village, surrounded by rolling green hills. It is situated below the main road, with its collection of grey stone cottages carefully placed around a small open square, which was once the village green.

In 1789 Edward Stillman became pastor of Keld and inherited a ruined chapel. Declaring that he would rebuild the chapel, he undertook a remarkable walk to London and back, raising £700 from preaching and begging. He deducted sixpence (2½p) from

this for his personal expenses. On his return he supervised the building of the new chapel where he completed forty-eight years as pastor to the people of Keld. The chapel, which is now the United Reform Church, was rebuilt in 1860 with the added features of a bell and a sundial.

The walk begins with a climb over the shoulder of Kisdon Hill, following a section of the old 'Corpse Road,' an ancient track once used for funeral processions. Before the church was built at Muker in 1580, the nearest consecrated ground was St Andrew's at Grinton, some 12 miles (19km) away. The corpse was carried in a wicker basket, by relays of bearers from villages along the way. The journey to Grinton could take up to two days. At intervals along the route there were 'coffin stones,' slabs of stone 6 feet (1.8m) long, where the bearers rested their burden.

Kisdon Hill, although only 1636 feet (498m) high, is still a very impressive mass of limestone, encircled with broken scars. It was formed during the last Ice Age, when glacial action widened the valleys and smoothed the hill tops. As the glacier melted a debris of rocks and clay blocked the valley, and the river Swale was diverted to its present course. This left Kisdon as an isolated rounded hill. Across the valley is the outpost of Angram, Swaledale's highest village at 1190 feet (363m).

On our descent from Kisdon there is a bird's eye view of Muker and the beautiful valley of the river Swale. After joining the Pennine Way we traverse the lower slopes of Kisdon Hill before descending steeply to Thwaite.

This picturesque village is where the famous Kearton brothers, Richard and Cherry were born. They were early wildlife photographers and lecturers at the start of the twentieth century. They used many ingenious devices to get closer to their subjects, sometimes concealing themselves in hollow tree trunks, and a papier mâché cow. This often blew over in high winds and apparently encouraged a bull! The house where they lived has a stone lintel above the door, decorated with animals and birds.

From Thwaite we follow the beck to Usha Gap Bridge where the road leads us to Muker. The Kearton brothers were educated at Muker and there are plaques on either side of the old schoolhouse door which commemorate them.

We leave Muker and follow a paved path through lush meadows, crossing the river Swale over Rampsholme Bridge. Here we join a riverside path and beautiful views of the river valley, surrounding hills and woodland are enjoyed all the way back to Keld. Along the way, a detour to visit the sad ruins of Crackpot Hall is highly recommended. The views extend down Kisdon gorge towards Muker and the course of the river Swale is clearly visible.

Crackpot Hall was built as a keeper's house by Lord Wharton. Herds of red deer roamed the hillside forests here up to 1725. Most of the forests where they lived were destroyed by fumes from the smelt mills and ground clearance for mining. The Hall is now just a ruin due to subsidence caused by the mine workings. Sadly the deterioration is getting worse, but the views of the gorge remain beautiful.

Start/Parking:	Keld village square. There is ample car parking available at Park Lodge Farm just off the village square.
Location:	Keld lies on the B6270 Richmond to Kirby Stephen road 12 miles (19km) west of Reeth.
Grid Ref:	893 012.
Distance:	6¼ miles (11km) circular. Allow 3½ hrs.
OS Maps:	Explorer OL30 (1:25,000) or Landranger 98 and 92 (1:50,000).
Refreshments:	Park Lodge Farmhouse at Keld. The Farmer's Arms, The Muker Store and Tea Shop at Muker.
Public Toilets:	Keld, half way between the road junction and the square, Muker, opposite the Farmer's Arms.
Other:	The United Reform Church, youth hostel, telephone, bus service.

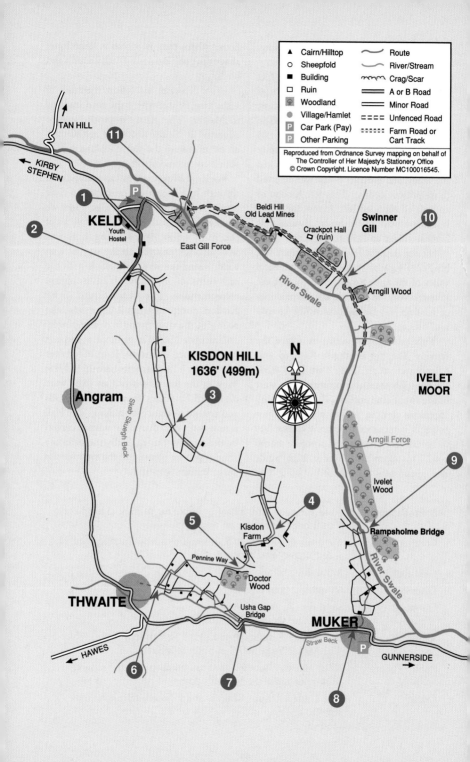

9 Kisdon Hill, Thwaite and Muker

1 *(GR: 893 012)* Leave the car park, turn right and follow the road up to the junction by the telephone box at the top of the village. Turn left towards Muker and Thwaite.

2 *(GR: 892 006)* After about ¼ mile (400m), take a track on the left *(SP Muker 2 miles)*. Follow the track down over the beck, go through the gate and climb up to the right. This track leads through four gates, over the shoulder of Kisdon Hill.

3 *(GR: 895 994)* At the fourth gate *(SP Muker)* continue uphill and go through a gate. Follow an enclosed section of track and go through another gate. The summit of the track is reached just before passing through the next gate. Keeping to the wall, descend through another gate to where the Pennine Way crosses.

4 *(GR: 903 986)* Turn right here towards Thwaite. Descend to Kisdon Farm and go through two gates to pass behind the farm to another Pennine Way signpost. Turn left here, continue through a gate and, after passing a small calf house, bear right to go through a gap stile.

5 *(GR: 900 983)* Continue down a narrow track passing a walled wood *(Doctor Wood)* and go through a stile next to a Pennine Way signpost. Keep to the left wall down to the bottom of the field and turn right to go through a gate, cross the bridge and the field beyond. At the next gate the path heads towards a stile, which leads into Thwaite village. Then retrace steps and continue from point 6.

6 *(GR: 894 982)* Turn left here and follow the path towards Muker. Keeping the beck to the right, go through two stiles then pass to the left of a barn, through two more stiles, over a bridge and a stile in the wall opposite. Turn right along the wall, through a stile and bear right to pass the front of a large barn. Follow the path through two gap stiles and a wooden step stile to reach the road by Usha Gap Bridge.

7 *(GR: 901 979)* Turn left and continue on the road to Muker.

8 *(GR: 910 979)* After passing the Farmer's Arms and the village store turn left, climb up past the church and village hall. Bear right and then left down a narrow lane leading to the Post Office, *(SP footpath to Gunnerside)* and continue through a gap stile. Follow a clear track through seven fields to reach the river bank.

9 *(GR: 911 986)* Turn right here, go through a stile and cross Rampsholme footbridge. Climb up a few steps and turn left. The path rises steeply at first. When it joins a well defined farm track, bear left and stay on the track to Swinner Gill.

10 *(GR: 909 005)* Cross the beck by the footbridge, go through the gate opposite and climb the steep track which levels out for about ¼ mile (400m)[1]. After going through a gate, the track descends gently to another gate.

11 *(GR: 896 011)* Go through the gate and cross a footbridge above East Gill Force. Turn left onto the Pennine Way and descend to cross a footbridge over the river Swale. Turn right and climb up a short rise to pass through an open gateway. Continue along this path which climbs to a junction. Turn right towards Keld, follow an enclosed path leading into the village square and return to car park.

1. *A detour can be made to visit the ruined Crackpot Hall and also the Beldi Hill Cairns which mark the site of the old lead mines.*

SLEI GILL and BOOZE MOOR

from Langthwaite 5¾ miles (9km)

Beginning from the cosy village of Langthwaite, this short walk has some outstanding views. Fine heather moorland and sparkling streams make up for the ravages of the lead mining spoil heaps.

Langthwaite is looked upon as the capital of Arkengarthdale and lies on the road from Reeth to Tan Hill. It was constructed in 1741 and was one of the first turnpikes. It was used for transporting coal from Tan Hill to be used as fuel for the smelting furnaces around Langthwaite.

Like many of the villages in Upper Swaledale, Langthwaite was a centre for the lead mining industry of the eighteenth and nineteenth centuries. However, in recent years the village has taken on a new role – in television. The Red Lion Inn is one

of the most televised public houses in Great Britain, having featured in the Yorkshire Television adaptation of Barbara Taylor Bradford's book, *A Woman of Substance* and its sequel *Hold the Dream*. Full length films such as Walt Disney's *Escape From The Dark* also featured the pub. Inside, apart from the usual treats, is a collection of books to rival many a bookshop. The village also provided the location for some episodes of the popular TV series *All Creatures Great and Small*. One sequence shows the vet's car crossing the bridge.

In 1656, Dr John Bathurst, who had been the personal physician to Oliver Cromwell, purchased Arkengarthdale from the Citizens of London. He began mining the area, naming the company CB after his son Charles. Between them they developed a thriving industry. At one time there were five inns, four alehouses, one church and six chapels tending to the needs of the 1500 people in the community, most of them working for the CB Company.

From the village square we follow the delightful Arkle Beck to Slei Gill, where we join an old miners' track.

The peaceful valley of Slei Gill with its attractive waterfalls, bears many scars from the lead mining period. All along the gill are deep-cut gullies or 'hushes' created in the early days of mining. At a merging of streams, the building which resembles a small limekiln is actually a wheel pit for one of the water-wheels, which powered the pumping and hauling machinery of the mines. The small arch is where the tail race came out.

Our walk continues above Slei Gill to join the Moresdale Road. From medieval times to the nineteenth century this track was part of a saltway. Salt was carried by packhorse from the Durham coast to the northern dales of the Yorkshire Pennines. It was also used in the opposite direction to carry lead eastwards to the coast

We remain on the track, following it across Booze Moor, passing some old mine workings and a line of bell pits.

Bell pits were vertical shafts which the miners dug to a depth of about 20 feet (6m) before digging horizontally, along the vein. Due to poor ventilation, these workings could not progress very far before the air became foul. There was also the danger of the tunnel collapsing. To prevent this happening another bell pit was sunk close by. This procedure was repeated many times, resulting in a line of bell pits spaced out along the length of the vein.

During our descent to Booze the scenery of Calver Hill, Fremington Edge and lower Arkengarthdale rouses the senses. Booze is a small hamlet, consisting of a few farms and cottages, but unfortunately no inn as its name suggests. As a matter of fact most of its early residents were Methodists and so they abstained from the demon drink. In 1473 the hamlet was known as Bowehouse changing through the years to Booze. The original name means 'The house by the curve,' the curve possibly referring to one of the nearby becks or to the curving hillside.

From Booze a narrow lane returns to the village square at Langthwaite. During the steep descent there are fine views of lower Arkengarthdale and a bird's eye view of Arkle Town with its old graveyard.

Start/Parking:	Langthwaite village square, there is a small car park and also limited parking in the village square.
Location:	Langthwaite is situated 3 miles (5km) north-west of Reeth on the road to Tan Hill.
Grid Ref:	005 025.
Distance:	5¾ miles (9km) circular. Allow 3 hrs.
OS Maps:	Explorer OL30 (1:25,000) or Landranger 92 (1:50,000).
Refreshments:	The Red Lion Inn and The Charles Bathurst Hotel.
Public Toilets:	Langthwaite, opposite the Methodist chapel.
Other:	Methodist chapel, St Mary's Church, Post Office, general store, telephone.

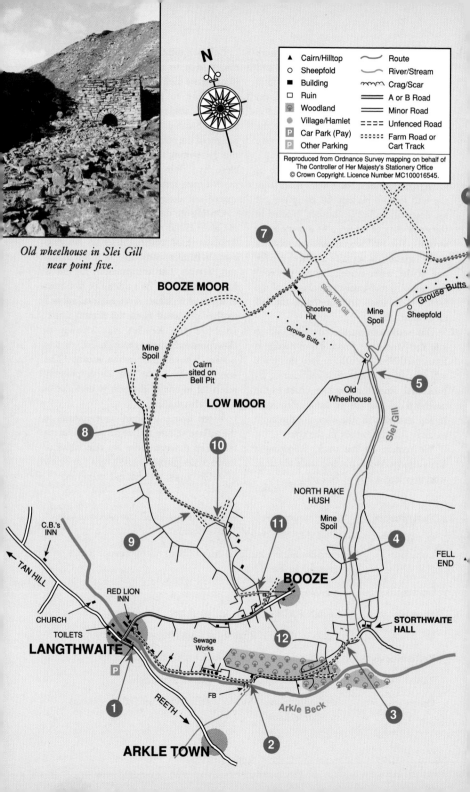

Old wheelhouse in Slei Gill
near point five.

Legend

- ▲ Cairn/Hilltop
- ○ Sheepfold
- ■ Building
- □ Ruin
- 🖼 Woodland
- ● Village/Hamlet
- 🅿 Car Park (Pay)
- 🅿 Other Parking
- ∿ Route
- ∿ River/Stream
- ⌢⌢⌢ Crag/Scar
- ═══ A or B Road
- ═══ Minor Road
- ==== Unfenced Road
- ┄┄┄┄ Farm Road or Cart Track

N

BOOZE MOOR

Slack Wife Gill

Grouse Butts

Shooting Hut

Grouse Butts

Mine Spoil

Sheepfold

Mine Spoil

Cairn sited on Bell Pit

LOW MOOR

Old Wheelhouse

Slei Gill

7

5

8

10

NORTH RAKE HUSH

Mine Spoil

9

11

4

FELL END

C.B.'s INN

TAN HILL

RED LION INN

CHURCH

TOILETS

LANGTHWAITE

🅿

BOOZE

12

STORTHWAITE HALL

Sewage Works

REETH

FB

1

Arkle Beck

3

2

ARKLE TOWN

10 Slei Gill and Booze Moor

1 *(GR: 006 024)* Turn right out of the car park, then take the first road on the right *(sign Red Lion Inn)* and cross the bridge over Arkle Beck. At the Red Lion Inn, turn right onto the lane opposite, bear right to join a broad track and follow the beck downstream.

2 *(GR: 011 021)* At a footbridge over the beck, the track bears left to run along the bottom edge of a wood. At a fork, bear left again *(SP Bridleway)* and climb to leave the wood through a gate. Follow the track to another gate.

3 *(GR: 016 021)* Go through the gate, continue straight ahead *(SP Slei Gill)* joining a clear green path which runs above the beck, through several fields.

4 *(GR: 018 025)* Cross over a wooden step stile and follow a derelict wall to an area of mining spoil heaps. Continue through the spoil heaps, passing North Rake Hush. The path joins the beckside and goes through a gate to reach a building with a small arch where two streams meet.

5 *(GR: 021 035)* Cross the stream in front of the building and climb up the hillside to the right. Turn right returning towards Slei Gill, follow a faint track through the heather to reach a line of grouse butts. Continue to the left of the grouse butts, *(the path remains vague)*. Near the last of the grouse butts the path heads slightly uphill and to the left. It eventually reaches a broad stone track. This is the Moresdale Road.

6 *(GR: 028 040)* Turn left and follow the track to a right bend, leave the track and continue directly across the moor to reach a stone track near a shooting hut.

7 *(GR: 018 041)* From the shooting hut continue along the stone track. After passing through the line of grouse butts, the stone track bends sharp right. Continue straight ahead on the left fork, which soon becomes a broad green path, eventually rejoining the stone track coming up from the right. Follow the track to reach a cairn, which is sited on a small mound or bell pit, and begin descending to reach a sharp right hand bend above a wall.

8 *(GR: 009 036)* Turn left here and follow a stony path through the heather. When the wall drops away to the right, continue straight ahead.

9 *(GR: 010 030)* Just before reaching a metal gate in a cross wall, fork left and head towards the left wall corner.

10 *(GR: 011 029)* Leave the track and follow the wall down and go through a gate/stile in the right wall. Keep close to the left wall down to the bottom of the field. Go through a metal gate, and, after about 10 yards (9m), bear left to join a green track between broken walls, which leads down to another gate.

11 *(GR: 013 025)* After going through the gate, continue to the left of a ruin, turn right and follow a farm track down to Booze.

12 *(GR: 013 024)* At the junction continue to the right on a rough road, which eventually becomes a tarmac surface and descends steeply down to the village square in Langthwaite. Continue over the bridge, turn left and return to the car park.

Information Desk

ABBEYS

Easby Abbey, near Richmond.
The substantial and interesting remains of this 12th century abbey are located in a beautiful position by the river Swale. It was founded by the one of the stricter orders, the Premonstratensian Canons.

CASTLES

Richmond Castle, Richmond.
This mighty fortress was built by William the Conqueror in the 11th century, to quell the rebellious North. Remains of the curtain wall and domestic buildings are combined with the 100 foot high keep added in the 12th century.

CRAFT CENTRES

Phillip Bastow, Cabinet Maker, Reeth.
Specialist in the design and manufacture of individual furniture commissions, using mainly oak, ash, elm and sycamore.

Joy Bentley Gallery, Reeth,
Painting and sculpture, visiting artists, pottery, painting, prints, silks, patchwork.

Pete Black Guitar Maker, Reeth.
Showroom open to guitar enthusiasts with twenty plus guitars always on view or available to play.

Clock Works, Reeth.
Creators and constructors of fine clocks and barometers. Repairers and restorers of antique and contemporary clocks and barometers.

The Garden House, Reeth.
'Garden House' pottery, also local patchwork and hand-knitting. Makers of and exclusive outlet for "Damson Cheese".

Greystone Studio, Gunnerside.

Pots 'n' Presents, Reeth.
Cottage shop offering traditional handthrown stoneware pottery, silver jewellery and lots of unusual gifts at affordable prices.

Old Schoolhouse Craft Shop & Gallery, Muker.
Serious sculpture, curious crafts, melodious music. A unique location.

Hazel Smith Gallery, Reeth.
Original paintings by Hazel and Vic Smith, showing the drama and beauty of the dales.

Shades of Heather, Reeth.
Traditional rug making - hooking, prodding and dyeing wools. Visitors by appointment.

Stef's Models, Reeth,
Animal figures and country wall plaques made from design stage to finished product.

Swaledale Woollens, Muker.
Unique cottage shop open all year round selling sweaters, cardigans, hats, scarves and gloves.

CYCLE HIRE

Dales Mountain Bike Hire, Fremington, Reeth.

H. S. Robinson, Kirby Stephen.

FARM VISITS

Hazel Brow Farm, Low Row.
Winner of Dales Environment award 1995. Farm visits and refreshments.

HISTORIC HOUSES

Aske Hall, Aske, Richmond.
The estate is at the gateway to the Yorkshire Dales on the outskirts of the ancient market town of Richmond. A Georgian coach house, with clock tower, houses the family's superb carriage which has recently been restored to its former splendour. There are also several follies including the Gothic style Temple, designed by Daniel Garret in 1745. The hall stands in Capability Brown landscaped parkland and overlooks a lake which serves as a natural wildlife sanctuary.

MUSEUMS

Georgian Theatre, Richmond.
A unique example of a Georgian Theatre with the majority of its original features intact. Built in 1788 by actor/manager Samuel Butler, it formed part of a theatre circuit which included Ripon, Harrogate, Beverley, Kendal, Ulverston and Whitby

Green Howards Regimental Museum, Richmond.
Set in a converted 12th century church, the museum's collection spans the 300 years of unbroken history of the Green Howards, one of Britain's oldest and most famous regiments.

Richmondshire Museum, Richmond.
This fascinating award winning museum presents the story of Richmondshire and its people. Transport in the Dales, mediaeval cruck house, James Heriot surgery set and local industry are featured.

Swaledale Folk Museum, Richmond.
The Swaledale Folk Museum depicts something of the way of life of the people of Swaledale, their farming implements, leadmining tools, pastimes and the impact of Wesleyan Methodism on their lives and thoughts.

OUTDOOR CENTRES

Marrick Priory Outdoor Education and Residential Centre, Marrick, Richmond.

Punch Bowl Leisure, Low Row.

RIDING & PONY TREKKING

Brookleigh Riding Centre, Eppleby, Richmond.

Arkle Moor Riding Centre, Arkengarthdale.

SWIMMING POOLS

Catterick, Catterick Garrison Camp Centre.

Richmond, Old Station Yard.

TOURIST INFORMATION POINTS

Barnard Castle, Woodleigh Flatts Road.

Kirby Stephen, 22 Market Street.

Reeth National Park Centre, The Green, Reeth.

Richmond, Friary Gardens, Queens Road.

Scotch Corner, Pavilion Service Area.

The Country Code

Enjoy the countryside and respect its life and works

Keep to public paths across farmland

Leave livestock, crops and farm machinery alone

Use gates and stiles to cross fences, hedges and walls

Guard against all risks of fire

Make no unnecessary noise

Fasten all gates

Take your litter home

Help to keep all water clean

Protect wildlife, plants and trees

Take special care on country roads

Keep your dogs under close control

Also . . .

Use car parks where possible and park with consideration for village residents and other road users.

Don't obstruct farm gates, tracks or entrances.

When walking on roads, walk on the right hand side to face oncoming traffic. When approaching blind bends, cross to the opposite side to enable you to see and be seen in both directions.

Allow sufficient time to complete the walk in daylight hours, and be sure to be off the fells by dusk.

Let people know the route you have taken, the time you expect to return and stick to the route.

If the weather turns nasty and you decide to quit the walk or take shelter in a hostelry etc., be sure to let others know so they don't worry and call out the emergency services unnecessarily.

Glossary

Many of the place names in Swaledale are Anglo-Saxon or Norse in origin. Anglo-Saxon names include those ending with *ing*, *ley*, *ham* and *ton*. Norse names include those ending with *by*, *sett* and *thwaite*. The Normans had a smaller influence on place names, being confined to changes in the spelling of existing names.

Aiskew:	*The oak wood.*
Angram:	*The pastures.*
Applegarth:	*Field with an apple tree.*
Arkengarthdale:	*The valley of Arkil's enclosure.*
Arkle Town:	*Arkil's farmstead.*
Aygill:	*The river in a ravine.*
Birkdale:	*The birch valley.*
Blakethwaite:	*Dark clearing*
Booze:	*The house on the curve of the hill.*
Calver Hill:	*The hill where calves are pastured.*
Calvert Houses:	*The calves' houses.*
Catterick:	*The hillfort, or the waterfalls.*
Cleasby:	*Kless's farmstead.*
Clints:	*The rocky cliff.*
Cogden:	*Woodcock valley.*
Copperthwaite:	*The cooper's clearing.*
Crackpot:	*The crevice where crows nest.*
Cringley Hill:	*The curving hill.*
Downholme:	*By the hills.*
Easby:	*Esi's Farm*
Ellers:	*The alders.*
Ellerton:	*The farm near the alder tree.*
Eskeleth:	*The hillside covered in ash trees.*
Faggergill:	*The sheep fold in the ravine.*
Feetham:	*The meadow.*
Feldom:	*The open land.*
Fremington:	*Frema's farm.*
Grinton:	*The green enclosure.*
Gunnerside:	*Gunnar's pasture.*
Harkerside:	*Harker is an old local surname meaning to eavesdrop.*
Healaugh:	*High forest clearing.*
Helwith:	*The ford made of flat stones.*
Hudswell:	*Hudel's well.*
Hurst:	*The wooded hill.*
Ivelet:	*Ifa's slope.*
Keld:	*Spring or stream.*
Kisdon:	*Small hill.*

Kirby Hill:	*Church farm.*
Kitley Hill:	*Hill near the cow valley.*
Langthwaite:	*The long clearing.*
Low Row:	*The low row of houses.*
Marrick:	*The ridge where horses graze.*
Marske:	*The marsh.*
Melbecks Moor:	*The streams by the sandbank.*
Muker:	*The small cultivated field.*
Old Gang:	*The old road.*
Owlands:	*Wolf grove.*
Oxnop:	*The valley where the oxen are kept.*
Rampsholme:	*The watermeadow where wild garlic grows.*
Ravenseat:	*Hrafn's hilltop.*
Ravensworth:	*Hrafn's ford.*
Rawcroft:	*The rough pasture.*
Raygill:	*The ravine.*
Reeth:	*The place by the stream.*
Richmond:	*The strong hill.*
Riddings:	*The cleared land.*
Satron:	*The wood cleared for pasture.*
Shunner Fell:	*The look-out hill, or Sjon's mountain.*
Skeb Sceugh:	*The wood where beehives are kept.*
Skelton:	*The farm on a shelf of land.*
Sleddale:	*The wide valley.*
Smarber:	*The butter hill.*
Storthwaite:	*The bullock clearing.*
Stubbing:	*The place cleared of tree stumps.*
Swale, River:	*The whirling, rushing river.*
Swaledale:	*The valley of the Swale.*
The Stang:	*The pole or stake.*
Thwaite:	*(Arkil's) clearing.*
Walburn:	*The foreigner's stream.*
Whaw:	*The enclosure with a sheep fold.*
Winterings:	*The meadows used for wintergrazing.*